We love jokes! We love history!

So we've put together a joke book full of history! Or is it a history book full of jokes?

There are jokes about cavemen for Jojo, about pyramids for Peewee, about gods with beaks for Grace and about Simon the brave cat for Stig.

Turn the page, get stuck in, and let the laughter start to rumble!

What's a snake's favourite subject?
Hisstory!

Why did all the cavemen go out at night?
To hit the clubs!

Which dinosaur had the biggest vocabulary?
The thesaurus.

SIR TONY ROBINSON'S

WEIRD WORLD OF WONDERS

JOKE BOOK

Hysterical, historical jokes & facts

Illustrated by Del Thorpe

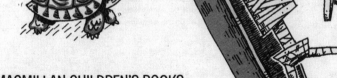

MACMILLAN CHILDREN'S BOOKS

With thanks to Jo Foster

Some material in this book previously published in the Sir Tony Robinson's Weird World of Wonders series titles *Romans* (2012), *Egyptians* (2012), *British* (2012), *Greeks* (2012), *Funny Inventions* (2013), *World War I* (2013), *World War II* (2013) and *Pets* (2014)

This edition published 2017 by Macmillan Children's Books
an imprint of Pan Macmillan
20 New Wharf Road, London N1 9RR
Associated companies throughout the world
www.panmacmillan.com

ISBN 978-1-5098-3880-6

A CIP catalogue record for this book is available from
the British Library.

Typeset and designed by Dan Newman/Perfect Bound Ltd
Printed and bound by CPI Group (UK) Ltd, Croydon CRO 4YY

Why can't you hear a pterosaur doing a wee?
Because the P is silent.

What do you do when a dinosaur sneezes?
Get out of the way!

What came after the dinosaurs?
Their tails!

Why was the archaeologist sad?
Her career was in ruins.

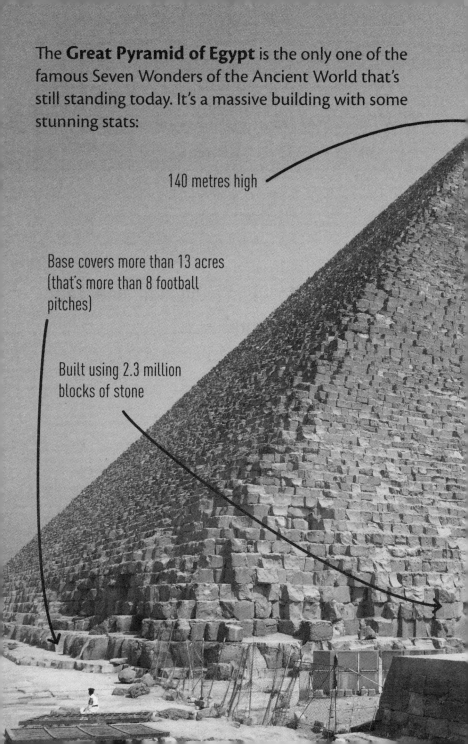

The **Great Pyramid of Egypt** is the only one of the famous Seven Wonders of the Ancient World that's still standing today. It's a massive building with some stunning stats:

140 metres high

Base covers more than 13 acres (that's more than 8 football pitches)

Built using 2.3 million blocks of stone

The Sphinx was probably painted in bright colours, but today the paint has worn off and the Sphinx has famously lost its nose and beard. That's what happens when you stand in the desert for 3,000 years.

VINTAGE JOKE ALERT!

This genuine Ancient Egyptian gag is one of the oldest recorded jokes in the world:

How do you put a smile on the face of a bored pharaoh?

Sail a boatload of young women dressed in nothing but fishing nets down the Nile and tell him to go and catch a fish.

What do you use to clean a pyramid?
Pharaoh liquid.

What do you call a pharaoh who's only 30 cm tall?
A ruler!

Pharaohs were so special that you weren't allowed to touch them – even if you accidentally touched a pharaoh's crown, you'd be put to death!

Which pharoah played the trumpet?
Tooting-khamun!

Not all pharaohs were men. The mighty **Queen Hatshepsut** ruled Egypt for fifteen years. But some people must still have had issues about women being rulers, because in order to encourage people to treat her like a man, she dressed in kingly clothes and even wore a fake beard!

Does my chin look big in this?

After the Greeks took over Egypt, pharaohs' names got a lot more boring. When Alexander the Great died, his Empire was divided up. One of his trusted generals, called **Ptolemy** (pronounced Tol-em-ee), took control of Egypt. He and his descendants are known as the Ptolemies because all the men in the family were called Ptolemy – Ptolemy the first, Ptolemy the second, Ptolemy the third . . . etc., etc., all the way up to Ptolemy the fifteenth!

EGYPTIAN CAT FACTS

(and you thought the internet was crazy about cats ...)

- In 525 BC, Persia attacked the Egyptian city of Pelusium. The Persian king knew how soppy the Egyptians were about cats, so he devised a plan: he ordered his soldiers to collect up loads of them, and just before the Persians charged, he released the moggies in front of his attacking army. Rather than run the risk of hurting the cats, the Egyptians immediately surrendered!

■ When an Ancient Egyptian pet cat died, its owners showed how sad they were by shaving off their own eyebrows.

■ Mummified cats were popular in Egypt, but so were other animals. Thousands of wild animals, like crocodiles, snakes and even fish, were mummified as offerings to the gods. You'd pop down to your local temple, pay for an animal to be mummified, and offer it to your favourite god as a kind of gift. A bit like when your pet cat brings you a dead mouse as a present . . . !

NILE FACTS

The Nile was a very big deal to the Egyptians. It was their farm, their supermarket, their builders yard and their playground. It was useful in all sorts of ways:

- It watered the crops so there was grain for making bread and beer.

- People drank and bathed in the water.

- Mud from the Nile was used to make bricks for building.

- Egyptians caught and ate the fish and birds that lived in and around the Nile.

- The plants that grew on the riverbanks were used to make boats, paper and even linen for clothes.

Hippos were a danger to anyone working, washing, or swimming in the river. The word 'hippopotamus' comes from the Greek for 'water horse', although they don't look much like horses to me.

USES FOR A MUMMY

Since ancient times, people have believed Egyptian mummies have special properties, so they've dug them up and used them for all sorts of things . . .

- **MUMMY MEDICINE** – Before there were medicines like aspirin and vitamin C, powdered mummy was thought to cure lots of illnesses. In the sixteenth century, King Francis I of France was said to take a dose of powdered mummy with rhubarb every day!

- **MUMMY PAINT** – Artists in the sixteenth and seventeenth centuries used a sludgy paint called 'Egyptian Brown' – made from powdered mummy bits!

- **MUMMY PARTIES** – In the 1840s and 1850s, mummy-unwrapping parties were popular in Europe. People came round to your house to unwrap a mummy, followed by drinks and nibbles.

What do you call a pharaoh
who tastes delicious?
A yummy mummy!

What did Hatshepsut say
when she had a nightmare?
I want my mummy!

I'm dead on my feet.

Why don't mummies go on holiday?
They don't want to relax and unwind.

How did some Egyptian writing
save a cliff from falling into the sea?
It was hero-cliff-fix!

You remind me of the Sphinx's face.
You mean beautiful and mysterious?
No - ancient and not all there!

What's a mummy's
favourite music?
Gangster wrap!

EGYPTIAN STYLE TIPS

■ Girls wore their hair in braids, or in pigtails hung with little weights to keep them straight, while boys shaved their heads except for a braided lock, which dangled down one side of their face.

■ For special occasions, some men and women wore wigs and hair extensions. Wearing a wig was a good way to stay cool – whenever it got too hot, you just took your hair off!

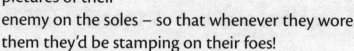

■ Most people went barefoot, but some had sandals with pictures of their enemy on the soles – so that whenever they wore them they'd be stamping on their foes!

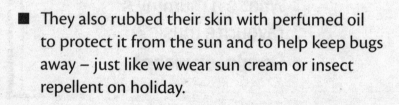

■ They also rubbed their skin with perfumed oil to protect it from the sun and to help keep bugs away – just like we wear sun cream or insect repellent on holiday.

- They painted bright green or black lines around their eyes, using make-up made from ground-up minerals mixed with oil. They believed this would stop their eyes from becoming infected and would reduce the glare of the sun.

- And they hung lucky charms called 'amulets' round their necks, ankles or wrists – amulets were precious stones carved in the shape of animals or insects, which they thought would keep away evil spirits.

TOP FIVE EGYPTIAN CURES

Egyptian doctors either had some funny ideas about medicine, or a really crazy sense of humour.

5 Baldness – Rub your head with a mixture of lion fat and various bits from a hippopotamus, crocodile, cat, snake and a big horned goat.

4 Grey Hair – Eat a mouse cooked in oil.

3 Whooping Cough – Eat a mouse roasted to a cinder and ground into a basin of milk.

2 Headache – Dab your head with the skull of a catfish fried in oil.

1 Infertility – Drink a mixture of dried, pounded dung beetles in water.

EGYPTIAN GOD FACTS

- The God **Osiris** was killed by his brother Seth and chopped up into little bits – luckily his wife Isis found the bits from all over Egypt and put them back together, and Osiris was OK again.

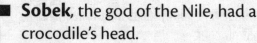

- **Tauert**, goddess of motherhood, had the head and belly of a pregnant hippo, because hippos were famously fierce mothers.

- **Sobek**, the god of the Nile, had a crocodile's head.

- To be pure enough to serve the gods, priests had to shave all the hair off their heads and bodies, and even pluck out their eyebrows!

- Priests could put a curse on someone by writing it on a piece of paper and then smashing or burning it.

EGYPTIAN WAR FACTS

■ When the Hyksos invaders arrived in Egypt, the Egyptians were seriously impressed with their wheels. Soon, pharaohs were using Hyksos-style horsedrawn chariots as status symbols as well as in battle. When King Tut died, six chariots were buried in his tomb – including a totally flash gold one.

■ After the Battle of Megiddo (around 1480 BC), the booty taken home by the victorious Egyptian army included 340 prisoners, 2,238 horses, 924 chariots, 200 suits of armour, 1,929 cows, 22,500 sheep, 87 knives, three kettles, and the King of Megiddo's tent poles.

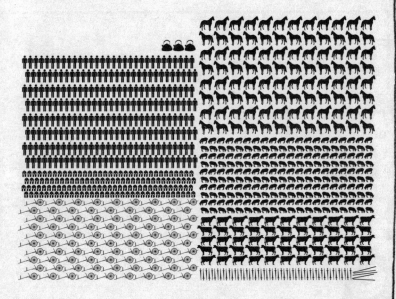

ALEXANDER THE GREAT FACTS

- **Alexander the Great** thought his own name was so great, he couldn't stop using it. He founded the new city of Alexandria in Egypt – but he also founded thirteen others with the same name. There were cities named after him in modern-day Turkey, Iraq, Pakistan, Afghanistan, Bulgaria . . .

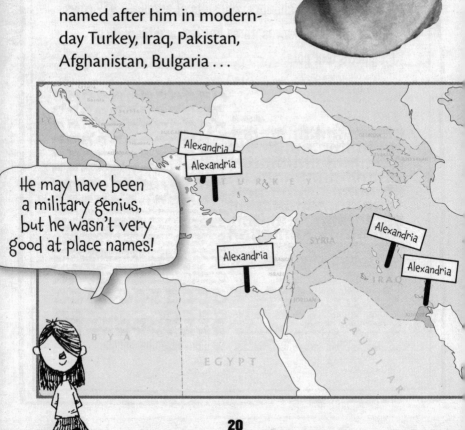

He may have been a military genius, but he wasn't very good at place names!

- Alex's horse had a big head so he called it Bucephalus (= ox-head). Eventually 'Ox-head' was killed in a battle. Alexander was gutted, so he founded a new city on the spot and named it Bucephala. The first (and only) city to be named after a horse!

- Alexander loved his horse so much that when Bucephalus was stolen, he threatened to destroy the whole country unless the horse was returned, which he promptly was!

- In India Alexander and his army discovered strange bendy yellow fruit growing on tall trees and they tasted delicious. In fact they were so yummy that the Greeks brought a load of them back home. So it's Alexander the Great that we have to thank for the banana!

OLIVE OIL FACTS

According to a story, the Athenians named their city after the goddess Athena to say thanks for her amazing gift of the most useful stuff ever: **olive oil**.

Ancient Greek uses for olive oil:

- Cooking
- Making salad dressing
- Burning in lamps, so you didn't have to go to bed as soon as it was dark
- Oiling athletes' naked bodies
- Offering to the dead as a present
- Washing yourself
- A mixing base for perfumes
- Curing diseases
- Giving as a prize to winning athletes. Winners of chariot races took home 5 tons of olive oil – that's more than 10,000 bottles!

TOP FIVE WAYS TO RULE

The Greeks had all sorts of exciting new ideas about how to run a society. In fact, we still use words with Greek roots to talk about different kinds of government.

5 Aristocracy = government by the best (or by the people who think they're the best!)

4 Democracy = government by the people

3 Tyranny = from **tyrannos**, an illegal or oppressive ruler

2 Monarchy = government by one single ruler

1 Anarchy = no leader at all!

PARTHENON FACTS

The Parthenon used more than 20,000 tons of gleaming white marble

Inside was a 40-foot statue of the goddess Athena. What's more, the statue was covered in gold – another 44 talents' worth!

No expense was spared: it would have cost you one silver talent to buy a massive warship – the Parthenon cost 469 talents!

The roof was held up by 48 giant columns

It's still there in Athens, but it's been knocked about a bit.

What was the most popular kids' film in Ancient Greece?

Troy Story.

In the 1800s, Lord Elgin came along and cheekily waltzed off with 75 metres of stunning marble sculptures. The Greek government have been trying to get them back for nearly 200 years.

GREEK VOTING FACTS

The Greeks were **crazy** about voting.

- The regular elections in Athens were so popular that the hill where they were held was called the Pnyx – which means 'crowded'!

- If Athenians didn't like someone, they could write their name on a broken bit of pottery called 'ostraka' and put them in an urn. If a person got more than 6,000 votes they had to leave the city for ten years. If they came back before their time was up, they were executed. This is where we get the English word meaning to punish someone by ignoring them or sending them away: ostracize.

- Athenians loved voting so much, they even voted on criminal trials. Huge juries of 500 people listened to a trial, then dropped metal discs into the jar for 'innocent' or 'guilty' to decide the verdict.

INNOCENT

GUILTY

JOJO'S LIST OF ...
TEN GREAT GREEK INVENTIONS

1 The First **Computer** – In 1900, divers
found a strange object in an ancient
shipwreck under water off the Greek island
of Antikythera (pronounced 'Ant-i-kithear-a'). It
was a machine about the size of a shoebox made of lots of little
rusty metal cogs and gears.

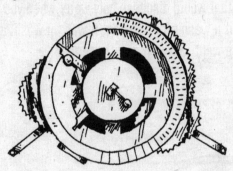

2 **Catapults** – The word 'catapult' comes from the Greek
meaning 'shield piercer'. The Greeks designed massive powerful
catapults – some of
which were wound
up and then released
two missiles
at once!

3 The **Alarm Clock** – Around 250 BC, the teacher Plato designed a water-clock with an alarm to help his students arrive on time to his lectures! It was made of a pot, which slowly filled up with water. When the level of water reached the top, it tipped a bowl of lead balls on to a copper plate and made a ringing sound!

4 The **Vending Machine** – Next time you're getting a packet of crisps or a can of Coke out of a vending machine, just thank the Greeks! The Greek inventor Heron of Alexandria designed a machine that would dispense holy water when you put a coin in a slot. But it wasn't for drinking; it was for washing your hands before you went to worship at the temple!

5 **Flamethrower** – This was a hollowed-out log, with a metal pipe running through it. At one end was some bellows and at the other was a cauldron full of flaming material. When you pumped the bellows, the air shot through the tube and blew fire at your enemy!

6 The **Alphabet** – Did you know that the Greeks came up with lots of the letters we use today? The word 'Alphabet' even comes from the Greek for A and B (Alpha and Beta).

7 **Automatic Doors** – Heron of Alexandria designed temple doors that opened automatically. At the same time, trumpets started to play, fog was pumped out and statues and metallic birds started singing.

8 **Secret Codes** – The Greek historian Polybius came up with a way of sending messages without writing them down. He invented a code that could be sent using fire beacons over long distances – each arrangement of torches signalled a different letter, and nobody watching would know what you were saying!

9 Death Ray – The Greek mathematician Archimedes (pronounced 'Arky-mee-dees') was a bit mad. They say he was once sitting in the bath when he had a great idea and was so excited he jumped up and ran through the streets naked, shouting 'Eureka!' ('I've got it!'). One of his most bizarre inventions was the 'death ray' – a series of mirrors that concentrated sunlight on to enemy ships and set them on fire!

10 Showers – And last but not least, the Greeks loved having a good scrub at the public baths and were the first people with showers . . . freezing cold ones!

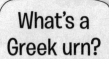

That's a Greek urn.

What's a Greek urn?

Not a lot. They're all skint!

That joke's even older than me!

What do you call a three-sided dinosaur?
A Pythagosaurus!

GREEK FACTS

■ The myth of the monstrous **Minotaur** who lived in the Labyrinth of King Minos might have had some truth behind it. In the rubble where the city of Knossos once stood, archaeologists have found the remains of a gigantic palace that would have been home to a powerful Greek ruler around 1500 BC. It's got more than 13,000 interconnecting rooms, passages and staircases – and lots of pictures of bulls!

■ Greek burglars were called '**wall diggers**' because they used to dig through the (mud) walls of houses to get inside and nick all the stuff!

■ Greek celebrity chef Archestratus wrote the first ever cookery book.

■ Brilliant Greek **Aeschylus** wrote the first proper play that still exists. He died when he was hit by a tortoise, which was dropped by a flying eagle . . . Honestly!

■ **Zeus'** favourite hobby was dating humans. He used all sorts of weird disguises to impress women, like swans, white bulls, eagles, showers of gold and flames of fire. Erm ... maybe no one told him 'hot' isn't supposed to mean literally on fire!

Hey, ladies ...
How you doing?

What did the Greek god do when he made a mistake?
He Apollogized.

Why did the Greek wrestler get the sack?
He just wasn't working out.

GREEK SCHOOL FACTS

- All Greek boys (girls didn't go to school) were expected to know the poetry of Homer. His most popular poem was about the war between the Greeks and the Trojans. It's over 15,000 lines long and would have taken about twenty-four hours to recite from start to finish.

- Greek boys had to be strong and athletic because they'd probably become soldiers when they were older. They went to gyms, where they were taught wrestling, running, jumping, discus and javelin throwing. But they couldn't get out of it by saying they'd forgotten their gym kit, because they had to do their exercises naked!

- At seven years old, all Spartan boys were sent away from home to be turned into soldiers. To toughen them up, each boy was given only one piece of clothing to wear and made to sleep outside even in winter.

What? I'm not bothered.

- Food was rationed, and boys were expected to steal to get extra food. But if you were caught you were severely beaten – although this wasn't to stop you stealing, it was to teach you to be a better thief!

- To celebrate getting to the age of twelve without starving to death or freezing to death, Spartan boys got to take part in a special challenge. Lots of delicious cheese was laid out on a table, but to reach the table you had to run past a lot of men attacking you with whips . . . I think I'd rather have had a nice party and some cake, wouldn't you?

GREEK FIGHTING FACTS

■ Greek soldiers were called 'hoplites' – which means 'armoured' – because they were dressed head to toe in heavy bronze armour. They also carried a large round shield covered in bronze called a 'hoplon'.

■ When the Battle of Marathon had been won, the Athenians sent their fastest runner – a chap called **Pheidippides** (pronounced

ATHENS
26 MILES

'Fi-dip-e-deez') – to take the news of their victory back to Athens. After legging it twenty-six miles, the exhausted Pheidippides arrived home, gasped 'We've won' and then dropped down dead . . . accidentally inventing the marathon race.

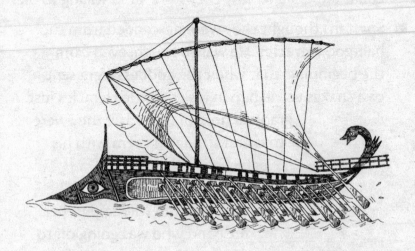

■ Before the battle of Salamis, the Athenians invested in 180 brand-new state-of-the-art battle ships. They were called 'triremes' or 'three-oarers' because there were three rows of oars on each side, powered by 170 oarsmen. On the front of each ship was a massive wooden battering ram to punch holes in enemy boats, and a pair of big white eyes to make them look extra scary!

EXTRA-TOUGH SPARTAN FACTS

- The food in Sparta was notorious – the most common dish was called 'Black Broth', and it was made of pig's blood and vinegar. One visitor to Sparta joked that having tasted Spartan food, he could understand why they were all so willing to die!

- Spartans thought they were descended from the half-god **Heracles**. He was so tough, even from the beginning, that when the goddess Hera sent two snakes to kill him in his cot, little Heracles just grabbed hold of them as if they were toys and strangled them with his baby fists!

- One Spartan wife said to her husband who was going off to war, 'Return carrying your shield or lying on it' – meaning either come back victorious or dead!

What is right in the middle of the Parthenon? **The letter H!**

OLYMPIC GAMES FACTS

■ Before the games started, the athletes would pray to Zeus that they would win their competition, and during the games one hundred oxen were sacrificed as a way of thanking him for being such a marvellous god!

■ A two-month 'truce' was held while the games were on, allowing people to travel safely to Olympia and back without having to go through a war zone.

■ One famous wrestler, **Milo of Croton**, won SIX Olympic titles! He was supposed to have eaten 20 lb of meat, 20 lb of bread, and drunk eighteen pints of wine a day. That's the equivalent of munching your way through forty massive burgers! He once trained for the games by lifting a newborn calf and carrying it about on his shoulders every day. As it grew, so did his strength. Eventually it became a full-grown bull, which he continued carrying about until he got fed up with it, then he slaughtered it and roasted and ate it in one sitting!

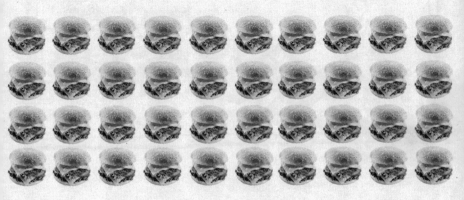

■ Disgraced cheaters were forced to pay hefty fines. Each fine paid for another statue of Zeus to be put up near the entrance of the stadium with the cheat's name on it in big letters– so that everybody would know what they'd done. Every athlete had to walk past these statues on their way to the games – how humiliating for the cheater!

JOJO'S GUIDE TO . . .
THREE OF THE MOST DANGEROUS (AND EXHAUSTING) SPORTS IN THE ANCIENT OLYMPICS

■ **Chariot Racing** – This was the Formula One of the Ancient World. Chariots pulled by horses sped up and down a track, careering around a turning post at each end. These posts were known as the 'taraxippus' or 'horse-terror' because it was here that most crashes took place. Accidents were often fatal – the drivers either being crushed by the chariot or trampled by the horses.

■ **Hoplite Race** – 'Hoplites' was the name for Greek soldiers. Contestants in the Hoplite Race had to run a race in full armour complete with a big heavy shield and a helmet!

■ **Pankration** – A combination of boxing and wrestling. The word 'Pankration' (pronounced 'Pan-krat-ee-on') meant 'total combat', and there were only two rules – no eye-gouging and no biting. The two competitors kept fighting until one was knocked out, gave up or died!

PERSIAN FACTS

■ The Persians created one of the largest Empires in history, covering a massive 8 million square miles and three continents. The word 'Persia' actually means 'Empire'.

What?

■ The Persians invented trousers! The Greeks wore a simple tunic, a bit like a T-shirt and skirt sewn together. But the Persian fashion was for baggy trousers tucked into their boots, because it was more comfortable for horse riding. The Greeks thought they looked ridiculous; as far as they were concerned, real men wore skirts!

■ The story goes that the Persian king **Xerxes** built a giant canal to invade Greece.

For a long time everyone thought it was just a story, as it wouldn't have been possible without modern mechanical diggers.

But using modern technology, scientists recently found evidence of the remains of it buried underground in northern Greece! Over a mile long and wide enough for two ships to pass, the canal must have been dug by hundreds of workers using just shovels and buckets on pulleys.

■ The canal allowed the Persian fleet to take a shortcut into the Aegean Sea. But after the invasion it must have silted up and become buried over time.

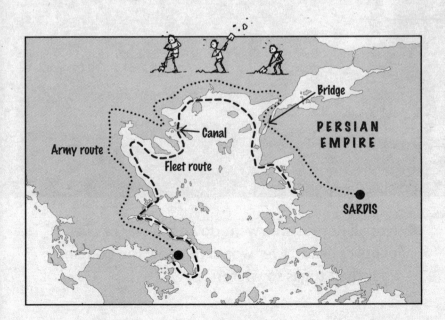

ROMAN PLUMBING FACTS

■ At one time Rome had nine aqueducts delivering 46 million gallons of water to the city every day. It collected in big reservoirs, then flowed through pipes into fountains, baths and private villas all round the city. Once it had been used, the dirty water from the streets, houses and toilets flowed back out of the city in sewer pipes.

The Pont du Gard bridge and aqueduct in southern France today

■ Not all Rome's wee went down a sewer or over people's heads. Ever wondered how the Romans kept their togas so white?

They sent them off to the fuller's shop to be washed, dyed, rinsed and dried. The chemicals in human urine are very good for cleaning cloth, so the fullers soaked people's clothes in vats of pee, which they bought from the city's public toilets!

■ The Roman Republic was really successful – all Roman citizens felt they had a say in how Rome was run and were really proud of it. And to remind everyone of that fact, the letters **SPQR** (which stood for 'Senatus Populus Que Romanus' or 'The Senate and People of Rome') were stamped not only on Roman coins, but on Roman buildings, Roman paving stones and even Roman drainpipes!

HANNIBAL FACTS

■ The Carthaginian general Hannibal was very good at coming up with sneaky and surprising ways to win. He'd won a battle at sea by throwing barrels of poisonous snakes into the enemy boats.

■ His most famous animal weapon was the war elephant: everyone knows Hannibal's army came to Italy over the Alps with elephants. Not everyone knows that many of them died on their trek through the snowy mountains.

■ War elephants weren't just unreliable; they were dangerous to get too close to. When the Romans attacked Carthage they blew loud horns to scare the war elephants – who then panicked and trampled Hannibal's own army!

Emperor: What's the weather forecast?
Soothsayer: Hail, Caesar!

Why did Hannibal go to Italy the long way round?
He wanted to keep the elephant of surprise.

Why couldn't Hannibal make shoes for his elephants?
Because it was an enormous feat!

ROMAN FIGHTING FACTS

- The Latin word for sword was **gladius** – which is where the word **gladiator** comes from.

- Roman soldiers took their training seriously: they practised with heavy wooden swords and shields, fought mock battles and even used the heads of dead cows as target practice.

- The Roman army was on the go from dawn to dusk, marching from place to place and pitching their tents at the end of each day. And when they weren't marching or fighting, the soldiers were building things like roads and forts.

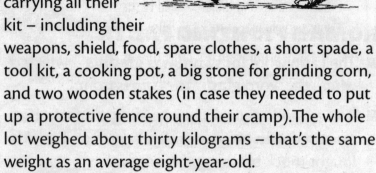

- They were
specially
trained to march
eighteen miles
in five hours in
full armour while
carrying all their
kit – including their
weapons, shield, food, spare clothes, a short spade, a
tool kit, a cooking pot, a big stone for grinding corn,
and two wooden stakes (in case they needed to put
up a protective fence round their camp). The whole
lot weighed about thirty kilograms – that's the same
weight as an average eight-year-old.

- If a whole unit fled from a battle, they were
'decimated'. **'Decimation'** means 'removal of a
tenth'. In other words, one in every ten soldiers was
picked out and slaughtered!

PEEWEE'S LIST OF . . .
ROMAN WEAPONS

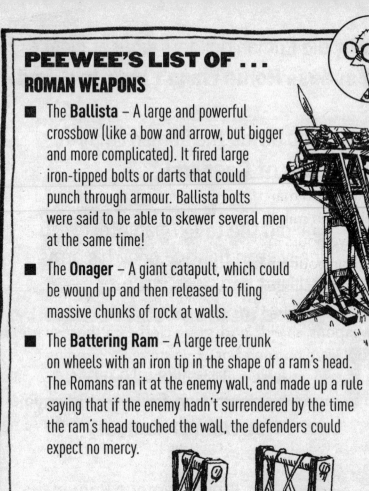

- The **Ballista** – A large and powerful crossbow (like a bow and arrow, but bigger and more complicated). It fired large iron-tipped bolts or darts that could punch through armour. Ballista bolts were said to be able to skewer several men at the same time!

- The **Onager** – A giant catapult, which could be wound up and then released to fling massive chunks of rock at walls.

- The **Battering Ram** – A large tree trunk on wheels with an iron tip in the shape of a ram's head. The Romans ran it at the enemy wall, and made up a rule saying that if the enemy hadn't surrendered by the time the ram's head touched the wall, the defenders could expect no mercy.

Why did Roman builders work at night?
Because Rome wasn't built in a day!

How do you divide the Roman Empire?
With a pair of Caesars!

Why did the tough gladiator finally stop fighting once his arms and feet had been cut off?
He was unarmed and defeated.

A Roman walks into a bar, holds up two fingers, and says:
'Five beers, please!'

Which famous Roman suffered from hayfever?
Julius Sneezer!

ROMAN FOOD FACTS

■ Romans' favourite flavouring was stinky fish sauce. It was called 'garum', and made of rotten fish guts. Boy, did it smell! But it was really popular and the Romans put it on everything, just like we splurge our grub with ketchup! Garum factories were often located far outside towns – I can't think why!

■ One Roman cookbook gives a recipe for baked parrot . . . and it says if you run out of parrots, you can use a flamingo instead!

■ For big feasts, cooks would stuff one animal inside another – maybe a chicken stuffed inside a duck stuffed inside a goose stuffed inside a pig stuffed inside a cow!

■ Romans liked joke food too; things like roast hare with wings attached to it, to make it look like a big flying rabbit!

MENU

SNAILS IN MILK

PEACOCKS' BRAINS

FLAMINGOS' TONGUES

EELS' INNARDS

BAKED DORMICE

STINKY FISH SAUCE

Actually, I'm not that hungry . . .

PET FACTS: BUNNY RABBITS

■ The Romans discovered wild rabbits in Spain and set up rabbit farms. Some people say that the name 'Spain' comes from the Latin word 'Hispania' meaning 'Land of the Rabbits'!

■ The craze for pet bunny rabbits didn't take off in the UK until Victorian times. Children were given rabbits as pets, and even adults took a fancy to them, breeding different types and entering them in competitions to judge which was the prettiest, or the fattest, or had the biggest ears.

■ One of Beatrix Potter's favourite rabbits was called Benjamin Bouncer, and she'd take him for walks on a little lead. She told people he used to rush into the dining room whenever he heard the tea bell, because he was so fond of the buttered toast on the tea tray.

PET FACTS: TERRIFYING RABBITS

■ In 1979 the President of the United States, Jimmy Carter, went fishing, and a giant swamp rabbit jumped into the water and swam towards his boat hissing menacingly. The president splashed at it with his paddle until it swam away. Next day a newspaper headline read: 'President Attacked by Rabbit!'

■ In 1807, the great military leader and French Emperor Napoleon Bonaparte held a rabbit hunt. Unfortunately the organizers used tame rabbits instead of wild ones and, when they were released, they ran back in the direction of the hunters looking for something to eat. Hundreds of them stormed towards Napoleon, who was forced to race back to his carriage to escape the horde of hungry hoppers.

■ In rabbit show-jumping events (yes, really!) the highest recorded jump by a rabbit is one metre, and the record for the long jump is three metres.

■ A mummy rabbit can give birth to up to forty baby rabbits each year. In 1859 the first twenty-four rabbits were brought to Australia. By 1959 the original twenty-four had become 600 million!

ROMAN FACTS

■ Roman kids learned to write on a tablet – a wax tablet, that is.

■ Romans didn't use the letters J, U, or W, and they didn't always put spaces between words, so Latin can look like gobbledygook even if we still use their letters and even some of the same words.

■ One in four people in the city of Rome was a slave!

ROMAN FIGHTING FACTS

■ **Tortoise/testudo** formation: Men stood in a square with shields round the sides and over their heads to form a protective shell. These shields were so strongly interlinked that it was said you could drive a horse and chariot over the top!

■ Another formation was called the **'wedge'**; legionaries formed up in a triangle, then the blokes at the front charged forward, with their swords driving the enemy line apart.

■ Most importantly, the Roman army always formed up carefully, quickly and in total **silence!** This took incredible discipline and would've been very off-putting for the enemy – it's a bit scary to see that the army you're about to fight is quietly getting ready to obliterate you.

HADRIAN'S WALL FACTS

■ Hadrian's Wall was so impressive that the Romans made souvenir mugs with pictures of the wall on them and the names of the forts round the rim!

■ It took the army eight years to build the wall. Well, it did stretch all the way across northern England.

■ One of the forts near Hadrian's Wall was called 'Vindolanda' (look at the map below), and in the 1970s a load of Roman wooden writing tablets were found there preserved in an ancient rubbish dump. They include fragments of letters from soldiers stationed on the wall, including birthday invitations and requests for more beer! They tell us that the

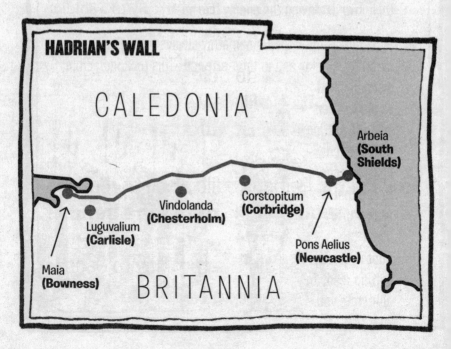

HADRIAN'S WALL

CALEDONIA

Arbeia
(South
Shields)

Corstopitum
(Corbridge)

Vindolanda
(Chesterholm)

Luguvalium
(Carlisle)

Pons Aelius
(Newcastle)

Maia
(Bowness)

BRITANNIA

Vindolanda fort has been recreated for visitors

soldiers called the local tribes 'The Brittunculi' or 'Little Britons' and that they missed the warm weather of home. One letter is a reply to a soldier who'd asked for more underpants!

What do Celts do when they don't like a vehicle?
They Boudicca.

Why did the Romans build straight roads?
So they wouldn't go round the bend.

What did the toga say to Caesar?
I've got you covered!

OMENS

Romans were always looking for signs to tell them whether the gods were happy or angry. These were known as **'omens'**. Before anything important was done in Rome – like passing a law or going to war – professional omen-readers were brought in to find out what the gods thought. They looked for omens in lots of things. For instance:

- **The weather:** When a storm blew up and thunder and lightning kicked off, they listened to it to try and work out what the gods were saying.

- **Animal guts:** A priest would cut open the belly of an animal to see if there were any signs from the gods in the shape and colour of its guts.

That doesn't look good . . .

- **Bird song:** They watched birds flapping about, and listened to them chirruping, because they believed that the birds were transmitting coded messages from the god Jupiter.

- The Roman army swore by omens too. They took **sacred chickens** with them into battle, and before attacking they'd choose one and crumble some food in front of it. If the chicken ate the food, it was a good omen; if it didn't, the omen was most definitely BAD.

In 249 BC before a sea battle, a sacred chicken refused to eat and the commander threw it overboard – saying if it couldn't eat, then at least it could drink! Of course, he lost the battle – which proves you should always listen to a sacred chicken!

I'm simply NOT hungry.

ROMAN FUNERAL FACTS

■ The dead weren't allowed to be buried inside the walls of a city, so the roads leading out were always lined with burials. This meant that people who wanted to go to a funeral had to go on a big hike.

■ The Romans loved a nice funeral and it was important to have a big procession. If you weren't very popular, your relations would hire some professional mourners who'd make a big fuss over you and make it look like everyone missed you!

■ Even slaves would put together the few pennies they had saved up to pay for a nice funeral. They knew that if they couldn't raise the cash, they'd get no funeral at all. Instead their body would be dumped in a pit on the outskirts of town at a grim place called 'Potter's Field', along with the local rubbish, dead animals and the scrapings off the road.

ROMAN EMPEROR FACTS

■ Julius Caesar's nephew **Octavian** was the first person to call himself 'Emperor', which meant 'Supreme Commander'. There were about 140 Roman Emperors in total. They were the most powerful men in Rome, with oodles of money and an army at their command. If you lived in the Empire you had to do whatever the Emperor said.

■ Crazy **Caligula** proclaimed himself a god and built a temple with a life-size gold statue of himself inside it. He raised taxes so he could roll around on piles of gold coins, and held lavish banquets where he drank pearls dissolved in vinegar. He even made his pet horse a senator and built him a big marble stable to live in!

- Emperor **Nero** used to put on shows where people were forced to sit and listen to him acting and singing for hours and hours. Some of the audience even pretended to be dead so they'd be carried out!

- Roman Emperors often wore special **purple robes**. Purple dye was very rare and expensive: only the rich could afford it. It came from a type of sea snail and you had to crush up thousands of them to get even a few drops of dye. The colour became known as 'imperial purple' and it was forbidden for anyone else in Rome to wear that colour. The sale of purple was even punishable by death!

SPORTS FACTS

- Not surprisingly, a chariot driver wasn't expected to live long – one celebrity driver called **Scorpus** won over 2,000 races before being killed in a crash when he was only twenty-seven years old.

- Some Romans would do **anything** for their team – at the funeral of one Red chariot driver, a Red supporter threw himself on the funeral bonfire along with the body.

- The **Colosseum** in Rome was a massive four-storey stone arena with tiered seats for 50,000 spectators. The word 'arena' means 'sandy place', because the floor was covered in sand to soak up all the blood.

The remains of the Colosseum are still standing in Rome today.

And the best seats were at the front, close to the action.

Crowds showed they wanted the loser to die with a 'pollice verso' – Latin for 'turned thumb'. But did that mean thumbs up, or down? No one knows!

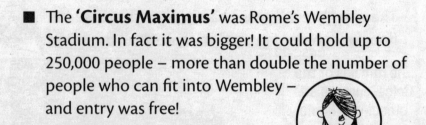

■ The **'Circus Maximus'** was Rome's Wembley Stadium. In fact it was bigger! It could hold up to 250,000 people – more than double the number of people who can fit into Wembley – and entry was free!

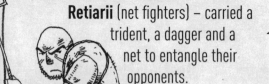

JOJO'S FAVOURITE GLADIATORS

Retiarii (net fighters) – carried a trident, a dagger and a net to entangle their opponents.

Sagittarii (archers) – mounted on horses and armed with a bow and arrow.

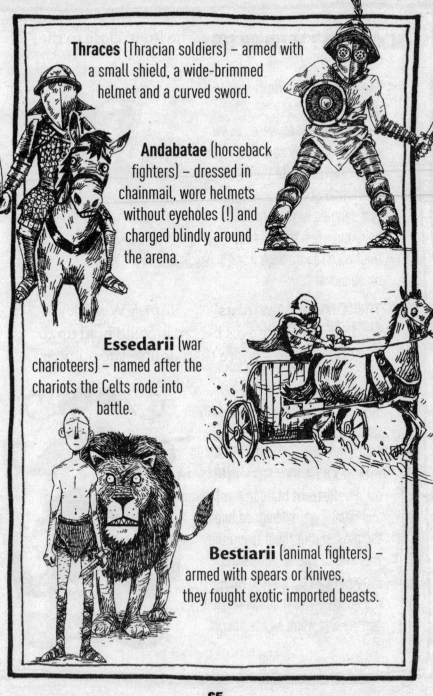

Thraces (Thracian soldiers) – armed with a small shield, a wide-brimmed helmet and a curved sword.

Andabatae (horseback fighters) – dressed in chainmail, wore helmets without eyeholes (!) and charged blindly around the arena.

Essedarii (war charioteers) – named after the chariots the Celts rode into battle.

Bestiarii (animal fighters) – armed with spears or knives, they fought exotic imported beasts.

MOUSTACHES THROUGH TIME

✂ The **Romans** couldn't stand moustaches. They thought they were unhygienic. They said that when the Gauls ate their meat, half of it got stuck and dangled in their facial hair, and when they drank, the booze ran through it like a sieve!

✂ **Victorian** men, especially in British India, sported all kinds of ridiculous moustaches, which were known as mutton-chops, handle-bars, nose-bugs, crumb-catchers, lady-ticklers and soup-strainers! The ends were curled, twirled or styled with wax until they stuck out like daggers. Dozens of little brushes and combs were designed to get the most out of them. There was even a special 'moustache spoon' with a lip on it to stop the gentleman's moustache from getting wet when he ate soup!

✄ Despite this, Victorians took their moustaches very seriously. The adventurer **Richard Burton** once challenged someone to a duel for insulting his moustache.

✄ When **World War I** began, it was a rule that all members of the British Army had to grow a moustache to make them look manly. Anyone found shaving their upper lip was severely punished.

✄ Eventually in 1916 this rule was dropped on the order of **Lieutenant-General Sir Nevil Macready**. This was partly because growing a moustache was a stupid thing to make people do, but also because Sir Nevil hated his own moustache so much.

It's like the small brushes with which kitchen maids and others clean saucepans.

What was the earliest British instrument?
The Anglo-Saxophone.

What newspaper did the Crusaders read?
The Daily Grail.

Why were knights so proud of their swords?
They were cutting-edge technology.

Where did knights learn to joust?
At knight school.

What do knights eat on their toast for breakfast?
Armourlade!

Which king liked his cheese in little bits?
Alfred the Grate!

Which Norman king was brown, shiny, and really, really hard?
William the Conkerer!

What was Alfred the Great's middle name?
The.

Why did Henry VIII have trouble breathing?
Because he had no heir.

TOP INVENTIONS: TELLING THE TIME

■ In 1585 a clockmaker in Germany made a clock mounted on a model ship. It could roll down the middle of a dining table, while a tiny pipe organ played a tune and the masts and sails twirled around until it came to a stop and fired eleven tiny cannon at the dinner guests!

■ Until the 1920s, men carried their watches on chains in their pockets – wristwatches were thought to be for girls.

■ Wristwatches in World War I became popular. Turns out that in the middle of a nasty battle, having a watch attached to your wrist was more sensible than having it waving about on a chain.

TOP INVENTIONS: LEONARDO'S GREATEST HITS

Leonardo da Vinci was an absolute off-the-charts genius who lived in medieval Italy. As well as creating world-famous art like the **Mona Lisa**, he came up with inventions that were way ahead of their time, including:

■ The world's first self-propelled vehicle. It was a three-wheeled cart, which worked like a wind-up toy – rotating the wheels backwards wound up springs inside, and when it was released the cart flew forward!

■ A giant crossbow.

■ A flying machine.

■ An eight-barrelled machine gun.

■ A submarine.

■ A tank.

■ A calculator.

■ A parachute.

UN-FUN EXPLORING

■ The Portuguese explorer Ferdinand Magellan spent over three months at sea without fresh food. His crew had to eat sawdust, bits of oxhide, and stale biscuits full of worms and soaked in rats' wee!

■ Christopher Columbus thought he might reach China after sailing west for a few days. After five weeks at sea, he ended up in South America. His crew must have been getting pretty tetchy!

I don't care what anyone says, I'm going that way.

■ The British colonists who set up camp in Jamestown, America, were soon so hungry they had to eat bits of old boot and tree bark to stay alive.

Why was Tudor England so wet?
Because Elizabeth I reigned for forty-four years!

Why didn't Shakespeare write Hamlet in pencil?
He couldn't decide between 2B or not 2B.

73

William Shakespeare walked into a pub.
The barman said: 'Oi! Get out, you're bard!'

What's a pig farmer's favourite
Shakespeare play?
Hamlet.

Which pirate says 'Arrr, QUACK, arrr!'
Francis Drake.

Why did the young pirate have to
walk the plank?
His family couldn't afford a dog.

What do pirates need to stay healthy?
Vitamin Sea!

Why couldn't the pirate
play cards?
**Because he was
sitting on the deck.**

Teacher: Grace, where on the map is America?

Grace: Here, miss.

Teacher: Well done. Now Jojo, who discovered America?

Jojo: Grace, miss!

How did the sailor fall in the sea without getting his hair wet?

He was bald.

ROYAL NAVY FACTS

- By 1815, the British Royal Navy had achieved its ambition, and had become the biggest and the best in the world.

- The largest ships in the Royal Navy were absolutely humungous – the biggest of them had three decks, one hundred guns sticking out of the sides, and over 800 crew members! (Which is probably more than all the people in your entire school.)

- The biggest ships had four and a half acres of sail; if you'd taken those sails down and put them side by side, they'd have covered more than two football pitches! And to hoist all those sails up the masts, they had twenty-six miles of rope, some of it thicker than your arm.

GRIM NAVY FACTS

■ Splinters were the commonest cause of death in battle in Nelson's navy. But we're talking **big** splinters!

■ Cannonballs could travel at 100 mph: fast enough to smash a wooden ship to bits.

■ Sailors who died at sea were usually sewn into their hammocks, with cannon shot to weigh them down, and the last stitch passed through their nose (to make sure they were really dead), before being dropped into the sea. But this didn't happen to Nelson – his body was put in a barrel of brandy to preserve it, then it was taken back to Britain, where he was given a hero's funeral in London.

GENUINE VINTAGE GAG

When Lord Nelson didn't want to obey an order at the Battle of Copenhagen, he held up his telescope and announced he couldn't see the flag signal. Of course he couldn't see it – he was holding the telescope to his blind eye! What a joker!

It was a navy superstition for every sailor to carry a bar of soap - so if he fell overboard, he could wash himself ashore!

TRAIN FACTS

- The slowest rocket: when **Stephenson's Rocket** won a race in 1829, it blew the crowd away with its top speed of . . . twenty-nine miles per hour!

- Some Victorian scientists said that your brain would stop working if you travelled at 20 mph, and predicted that anyone going at more than 30 mph would have all the air sucked out of them and would suffocate to death.

- By 1845 there were over 2,000 miles of railway track in Britain, and 30 million passengers were travelling by train each year!

■ The first person to be run over by a train was a VIP guest, the MP **William Huskisson**. He was killed at the grand opening of the Liverpool to Manchester railway.

How can you tell where a train's come from? By its tracks.

Ticket inspectors are great, aren't they? You've got to hand it to them.

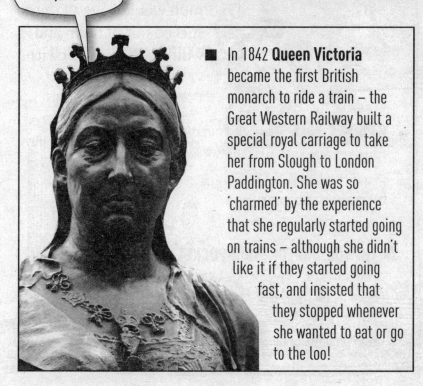

Stop the train! One needs a wee.

■ In 1842 **Queen Victoria** became the first British monarch to ride a train – the Great Western Railway built a special royal carriage to take her from Slough to London Paddington. She was so 'charmed' by the experience that she regularly started going on trains – although she didn't like it if they started going fast, and insisted that they stopped whenever she wanted to eat or go to the loo!

TOP FIVE WEIRD THINGS IN THE GREAT EXHIBITION

5 DR GEORGE MERRYWEATHER'S TEMPEST PROGNOSTICATOR A weather-forecasting gadget, made up of twelve glass bottles each containing a leech, which were connected to a small bell using various wires, chains and bits of whalebone. When the leeches sensed a change in the atmosphere, they were supposed to climb up their bottles and trigger the bell.

4 THE ALARM CLOCK BED The inventor Theophilius Carter came up with an ingenious 'silent alarm clock bed' – a clockwork bed that tipped its occupant out on to the floor at the appointed time!

3 THE TOO-BIG-FOR-YOUR-POCKET PENKNIFE One Sheffield cutler went totally over the top for the Exhibition and made a gigantic two-and-half-foot-long pocket-knife with seventy-five blades, saws, hooks, picks and assorted gadgetry, all engraved with pictures of famous buildings and people.

2 **LIEUTENANT HALKETT'S INDIA RUBBER BOAT-CLOAK** This magnificent and bizarre invention was a rubber cloak that could be pumped up with bellows stored in one pocket, and steered with paddles stored in the other!

1 **MONKEY CLOSETS** Some of the first public toilets (or 'monkey closets' as they were known) were installed at the Great Exhibition. More than 800,000 people paid a penny to use them – which is where the term 'spend a penny' comes from! Unfortunately, once you were inside you had to keep one hand firmly on the door handle, because they didn't have locks. The vacant/engaged bolt wasn't invented until thirty years later!

Crikey, is this the queue for the loo?

TOP INVENTIONS: TOILETS THROUGH TIME

■ The **flushing toilet** may be over 5,000 years old – experts studying the remains of a Stone Age village on the Orkney Islands in Scotland found that the houses contained little closets with drains underneath that were flushed by the nearby river!

■ **Roman toilets** could seat up to sixty people – yikes!

■ Before flushing loos were introduced, boys were employed as **'gong scourers'** ('gong' was an old word for toilet) – their job was to clean the sewers and chambers underneath toilets and stop them getting blocked up. They spent hours up to their

necks in other people's poo and sometimes passed out from the smell.

- In 1861, crafty plumber **Thomas Crapper** started making and selling flushing toilets – he encouraged lots of people to buy one for their homes.

- The first **packaged toilet paper** was made in America in 1857, and in 1880 the British Perforated Paper Company created paper that came in boxes of pre-cut squares. Loo rolls didn't become common until 1907.

How many witches does it take to change a light bulb?

What do you want it changed into?

How many tourists does it take to change a light bulb?

Six. One to hold the bulb and five to ask for directions.

How many film stars does it take to change a light bulb?

One, but he only takes one step up the ladder, and then his stunt double takes over.

INTREPID VICTORIAN EXPLORERS

RICHARD BURTON

Special interests: Wide-ranging. He was a soldier, spy, explorer, writer (one of his books is a history of farting), translator who spoke over twenty-five languages, poet, and amateur hypnotist!

Style: Master of disguise.

Daring escape: Once he was attacked by Somali warriors, and a javelin went straight through his mouth. Incredibly, he remained conscious and managed to make his escape with the weapon still sticking out of him!

MARY KINGSLEY

Special interests: Biology. Collects exotic fish and snakes for museums.

Style: The Africans must have thought she looked pretty weird, hacking her way through the jungle dressed exactly like she would have back home, in a long black skirt, a black shawl and a black bonnet.

Daring escape: One day she accidentally trod on an animal trap, and fell fifteen feet into a deep pit lined with twelve-inch wooden spikes. But her huge skirt cushioned her fall and she survived with only a few bruises!

DAVID LIVINGSTONE

Special interests: Medicine, religion, finding the source of the Nile.

Style: Classic British gent.

Daring escape: Surviving pneumonia, malaria, cholera, dysentery, and horrible foot ulcers when trekking around Africa. He even lived through a lion attack.

Livingstone's far-flung parts: When journalist Henry Morton Stanley finally found him, the explorer refused to give up his mission and return home – he was still determined to find the source of the Nile. He never did, though, and he died in Africa in 1873. After his death, Livingstone's body was buried in Westminster Abbey, but his heart was buried separately in Africa, the continent he loved.

INFLUENTIAL INDIA

■ The British who lived in India came back home with quite a few native words we still use today. If you ever find yourself in a **bungalow**, and decide to take off your **dungarees** and put on your **pyjamas**, you'll be using three words that come from India. (Although whose bungalow it'll be, and why you'll be going to bed in it, I have no idea!)

■ After the Indian Mutiny in 1857, many British soldiers stopped wearing obvious red jackets and dyed their white shirts with tea to make them 'khaki' colour (**khaki** is Persian for 'dust').

■ The first Indian restaurant in London, 'the Hindoostanee Coffee House', was opened in 1809.

A FEW OF VICTORIA'S FAVOURITE THINGS

Queen Victoria made the most of the fun bits of being queen, and when she found something she liked she could be very enthusiastic.

Things Victoria loved include:

ALBERT'S MOUSTACHE: She wrote in her diary about how 'excessively handsome' he was and how she liked his 'delicate moustachios, and slight but very slight whiskers'.

THE GREAT EXHIBITION: Victoria was such a fan, she visited thirty-three times in five months – and she said the opening day was the happiest day of her life.

CURRY: Victoria employed her very own Indian servant who cooked the Queen's curries just the way she liked them.

LET'S CALL IT . . . VICTORIA!

Queen Victoria ruled for sixty-two years, and had a huge empire that covered a quarter of the world. So there were thousands of people who wanted to suck up to her – and a popular way to do it was to name something after her. Which is why all these things have the same name:

- **Victoria Falls** (previously known as 'Smoke That Thunders') in Zambia
- **Victoria**, a state in Australia
- **Victoria**, capital city of the state of British Columbia, Canada
- **Lake Victoria**, the largest lake in Africa
- **Victoria**, capital city of the Seychelles
- **Victoria Station** in London
- **The Victoria and Albert Museum** in London
- **Victoria sandwich** (the cake!)

There wasn't enough room on the page to include everything named after Queen Victoria. Can you think of any more? Maybe there's a Victoria Road near you . . .

What did Queen Victoria say
to the knock-knock joke?
'We are not amused.'

What did Queen Victoria say
when she solved the riddle?
'We are not bemused.'

What did Queen Victoria say
when she went barefoot?
'We are not in shoes.'

What did Queen Victoria use her throne for?
The royal wee!

What did Queen Victoria do when she burped?
She issued a royal pardon.

Where was Queen Victoria crowned?
On her head!

Why didn't anyone invest in the first aeroplanes?
They didn't think they would take off.

Have you heard the joke about the first aeroplane?
You won't get it – it will go right over your head.

Why did the Prime Minister
have tired legs?
**Because he had to stand
for election.**

I know every single detail of the
first camera ever invented.
**You could say I've got a
photographic memory.**

Why can't a bicycle stand up?
Because it's two tyred.

NEW RECRUITS

■ When Lord Kitchener advertised for men to join the Army, even he was surprised by how keen people were. Kitchener had thought he'd be able to recruit 100,000 soldiers, but within two months a massive 750,000 had volunteered! By the end of World War I over 5 million British men had joined the army.

Which British General cooked the best breakfast?
General Kitchener!

Where did the German Kaiser keep his armies?
Up his sleevies!

"YOUR COUNTRY NEEDS **YOU**"

- It wasn't just men who joined up; plenty of boys did as well, some as young as twelve! To fight abroad, soldiers were supposed to be over nineteen, but lots of boys lied about their age.

- Some eager lads wore their Sunday suits or their dad's clothes to make them look older. Others gave fake names so that their parents wouldn't be able to find them and drag them back home.

- Women weren't allowed to be soldiers, but that didn't stop nineteen-year-old Dorothy Lawrence. When she was told she couldn't go to the front as a war reporter, she got hold of an army uniform, cut her hair and cycled to the front line with forged ID papers, which said she was Private Denis Smith! Unfortunately ten days later she was discovered and sent back home.

WARNING: GENUINE VINTAGE WORLD WAR I JOKE

Commander: 'Number One! Why don't you hold your rifle properly?'

Soldier: 'I've got a splinter in my hand, Sir!'

Commander: 'Been scratching your head, I suppose!'

TRENCH FACTS

■ World War I armies wanted their trenches to be a zigzag shape, not one long line. That way, if the enemy managed to get in it, they wouldn't be able to shoot all the way down it and kill everybody at once. And if a bomb hit, the explosion wouldn't blow everyone up!

- There were over 25,000 miles of trenches stretching from the English Channel all the way to Switzerland.

- To make sure the soldiers didn't get lost, signposts were put up, and the trenches were given names like 'Rats' Alley', 'Casualty Corner' and 'Deadman's Ditch'!

- On night raids soldiers blackened their faces with burnt cork, and carried weapons that didn't make any noise, like clubs, knives, hatchets and brass knuckles (lumps of metal that fitted over your fingers so you could give your enemy a killer punch).

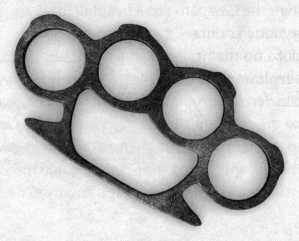

WORLD WAR I FACTS

■ Soldiers in the trenches often ate World War I ready meals: tinned food, which had been invented in the nineteenth century as a way of keeping food fresh. Meals included corned beef, Irish stew, and pork and beans. The French army had tinned chicken in wine, and the Italians were given tinned spaghetti Bolognese!

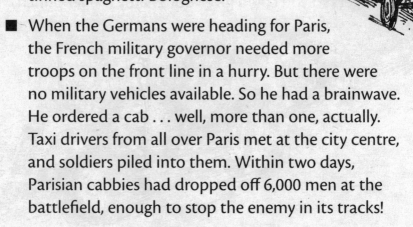

■ When the Germans were heading for Paris, the French military governor needed more troops on the front line in a hurry. But there were no military vehicles available. So he had a brainwave. He ordered a cab . . . well, more than one, actually. Taxi drivers from all over Paris met at the city centre, and soldiers piled into them. Within two days, Parisian cabbies had dropped off 6,000 men at the battlefield, enough to stop the enemy in its tracks!

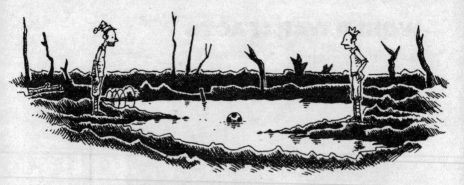

On Christmas Day 1914, a big truce took place along large parts of the front line. German soldiers put up little Christmas trees along their trenches, and both sides sang carols and shouted 'Merry Christmas' to each other. Some soldiers got out of their trenches and exchanged cigarettes and presents! A few even got together and played a game of football in no-man's-land, with helmets for goalposts.

Hurry up, guys. I'm starving!

GREAT INVENTIONS: TINNED FOOD

■ The famous French general Napoleon Bonaparte was so fed up of his soldiers' food going off that in 1795, he offered a prize of 12,000 francs to anyone who could invent a way to keep food fresh for longer. A French chef called Nicholas Appert won the prize when he discovered you could keep food fresh if you sealed it tightly in a glass container and then boiled it.

■ In 1810, brilliant British inventor Peter Durand designed a more robust metal container – the first tin can! And thirty years later, Henry Evans invented a machine that could produce sixty tin cans an

WHOLE SQUID | JELLIED EELS | FULL BREAKFAST | SHARK FIN SOUP | SNAILS

CREAMED POSSUM | HAGGIS | ROAST CHICKEN | ROASTED SCORPION | CHEESE BURGER

hour – soon people were using tin cans to store everything from oysters to spaghetti Bolognese.

■ Getting the food out of the tins was tricky though – you had to use a hammer and chisel until the first tin opener was invented in 1858!

■ The famous explorer Sir John Franklin and his team took 8,000 tins of food with them on their expedition to the Arctic in 1845 (just imagine having to eat tinned food for three years!). Unfortunately one of the things used to make their cans was lead, and that's poisonous. For some reason, they never made it back from the Arctic . . . !

WORLD WAR I SLANG

Ordinary British soldiers had their own special language. Here are some key words . . .

Blighty – Britain. From the Hindu word 'Vilayati', meaning 'foreign'. Originally used by British troops in India. Later a 'Blighty' meant a wound so bad that it would get you sent home.

Boche – A German soldier. From the French 'caboche', meaning 'blockhead'!

Brass Hat – A high-ranking officer. Officers often wore a brass-coloured braid on their hats.

Bully Beef – Canned corned beef found in ration packs. From the French 'bouilli' meaning 'boiled'.

Hun – Another word for a German soldier. The original Huns were a tribe from Asia who attacked Europe in the fifth century. In a speech in 1900 Kaiser Wilhelm compared the German Army to the Huns, and it quickly became their nickname.

Kraut – Yet another word for a German soldier. Short for 'sauerkraut' which means 'pickled cabbage' (a dish that the Germans found very tasty).

Napoo – Dead, as in, *'If we don't get out of here fast, we'll all be napoo.'* From the French phrase *'Il n'y en à plus'* meaning *'There isn't any more'*, which the British thought sounded like *'napoo'*.

Old Sweat – An experienced soldier.

Tommy – A British soldier. Came from the name 'Tommy Atkins', which was used as an example name on British Army forms, a bit like 'Joe Bloggs' today.

Trench Rabbit – A rat.

STIG'S WEAPONS FACTS

■ Both sides used weapons called shells: hollow cannonballs filled with explosives and sometimes with small pieces of metal called shrapnel.

I love enormous shells!

You wouldn't love these!

■ The most famous German super-gun, Big Bertha, weighed as much as four double-decker buses! Her shells were the size of dustbins, they weighed over 900 kg, and she could fire them nine miles – high enough and far enough to go right over Mount Everest!

■ Women back in Britain did the dangerous job of filling shells with explosive powder. These women were known as 'canaries', because the explosive turned their skin bright yellow. It was extremely poisonous and made you so sick you could die.

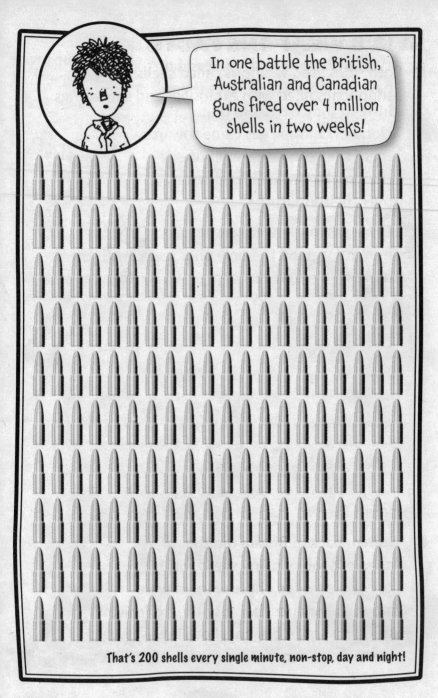

- Chlorine gas was a new weapon in World War I. At first soldiers didn't have gas masks to protect them. Instead they were told that if a cloud of chlorine gas came towards them they should take off one of their socks, pee on it and put it over their mouths!

I do that too sometimes!

- Once gas masks were developed, humans weren't the only ones issued with them – horses, dogs and carrier pigeons got them as well!

SUPERNUMBERS

World War I was so huge that all sorts of things happened on a more massive scale than ever before. Try to wrap your head around some of these numbers:

In August 1914 the French Army lost **211,000 men** in sixteen days.

In 1915 nearly **2 million** Russian soldiers died or were badly hurt.

In June 1916 the Austro-Hungarian Army suffered **280,000 casualties** in one week.

On the first day of the Battle of the Somme in July 1916, **60,000** British soldiers died or were injured. This is the highest number of men killed on any single day in the history of the British Army.

In 1916 alone the German Army lost **1.4 million men**.

The Russians had 6.5 million men, but only 4.5 million rifles. By 1916 the Russian Army had lost more than **two million men!**

By the end of the war **21 million men** had been seriously wounded.

TANK FACTS

- Tanks were first used in battle by the British in 1916. The inventors of tanks were inspired by . . . tractors! They're basically a bulletproof tractor with a gun on the front.

- At first, the new invention was called the Landship. But that was too obvious – if the Germans heard about a Landship they'd know what was up. So instead, someone commented that the Landship looked more like a water tank – and the name stuck.

■ When the Germans finally realized what the Allies were up to, they tried to develop tanks too . . . but it was too late. By the end of the war the British and French had built over 5,000, while the Germans had only twenty!

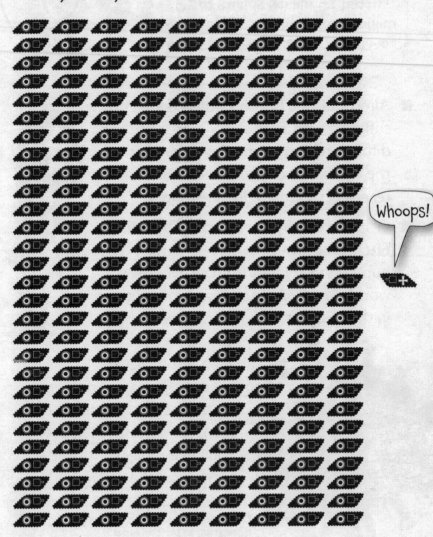

GRACE'S MEDICAL FACTS

Between 1914 and 1918 British doctors used 108 million bandages and 7,250 tons of cotton wool, fitted 1.5 million splints to 1.5 million broken limbs, and inserted over 20,000 artificial eyes into 20,000 eye sockets!

- Almost 80,000 British soldiers ended up suffering with 'shell shock', and it was very difficult to cure them. Ten years after the war finished, 65,000 men were still receiving treatment for shell shock.

- In 1918 a deadly disease called **Spanish Flu** hit the armies of Europe. Large numbers of soldiers from all over the world were living in unhealthy conditions in the trenches. This helped spread the flu virus really quickly. Soldiers caught a terrible fever and died within days. Armies on both sides lost thousands of men. Spanish Flu killed over 50 million people worldwide – more than the war itself!

The flu virus looks something like this (though not as big, obviously)

TOP THREE MEDICAL INVENTIONS OF WORLD WAR I

1 BLOOD BANKS: At the start of the war, if someone needed a blood transfusion, doctors needed to take the blood straight from the donor's arm. Eventually one doctor had the bright idea of collecting it in special bottles on ice, and transporting them to hospital tents near the front line. He'd invented the first blood bank!

2 MODERN PLASTIC SURGERY: Surgeon Harold Gillies transformed plastic surgery during the war. But if a man's face was too badly damaged for this kind of treatment, Gillies fitted a metal mask over his face, which was painted to match his skin colour. Fake eyebrows, eyelashes and a moustache were then glued on to it using real hair. These masks were made in a workshop in a London hospital known as the 'Tin Noses Shop'.

3 GUIDE DOGS FOR THE BLIND: The idea of guide dogs was invented by German doctor Gerhard Stalling – or rather, by Dr Stalling's dog. Dr Stalling treated soldiers who had been blinded. One day he left his dog with one of his patients. When he returned, he realized the dog was trying to look after the poor man. Did this mean that dogs might be able to help the blind? Stalling started training them and had amazing success. In 1916 he opened the first ever guide-dog school, and by the end of the war his schools were training 600 dogs a year!

PETS AT WAR

- One of the greatest hero pets was called **Sergeant Stubby**! He was a pit bull terrier. But when he became part of a regiment of American soldiers in World War I... he turned into a superhero! He found wounded soldiers, he warned his unit when he smelt poison gas or heard falling bombs. He caught a German spy by biting him on the leg and making him fall over! He took part in seventeen battles and won lots of medals for bravery.

Our hero!

My hero!

- **Simon the Cat** served on a Royal Navy warship during World War II. He helped to keep the sailors happy by purring, playing, and generally being cute. He also stopped the ship being overrun with rats. He was badly injured during an enemy attack, but survived and became a celebrity back in Britain.

- **Rip the Terrier** was found wandering round London by an Air Raid warden during World War II. He became one of our first search-and-rescue dogs and sniffed out people who were trapped under fallen buildings after explosions. In just one year he rescued over a hundred casualties!

- **Commando** was one of about 250,000 pigeons who served in World War II. Commando made more than ninety trips into occupied France with a little canister tied to his leg full of top secrets. He flew all the way there and back, dodging German guns and birds of prey, which had been trained by the Germans to kill messenger pigeons.

PEEWEE'S GUIDE TO SOLDIERS' STUFF

Each army gave its soldiers slightly different bits and pieces to carry, but most of them were kitted out with . . .

A GAS MASK In case of a gas attack. They were heavy, were hardly ever needed and lots of soldiers left them behind or pretended they'd lost them.

RATIONS Soldiers in the field mostly lived on tinned beef, biscuits and the odd bit of chocolate. American soldiers were given packets of M&Ms.

A HOUSEWIFE No, not a tiny woman you put in your pocket. It was the soldiers' name for a sewing kit. It was for mending rips in your clothing and generally stopping all your clothes falling off.

A RIFLE This was a gun with a long barrel that was so accurate it could hit an enemy up to 300 metres away.

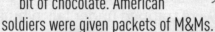

A BAYONET If you missed, you could screw this handy dagger-like attachment on the end of your rifle, run up to your enemy and stab him!

SPARE SOCKS You'd sell your granny for a nice dry pair of these.

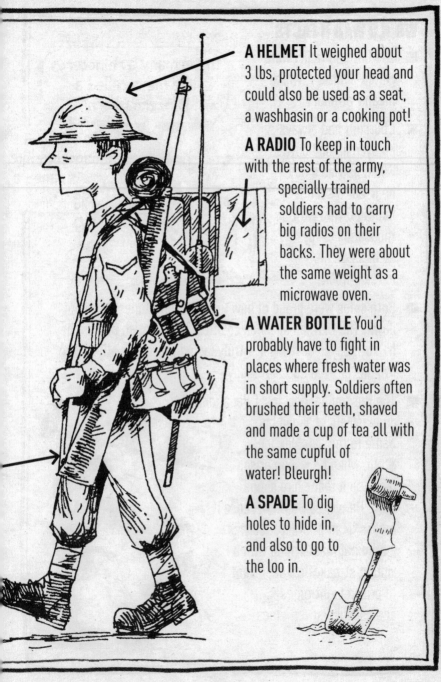

A HELMET It weighed about 3 lbs, protected your head and could also be used as a seat, a washbasin or a cooking pot!

A RADIO To keep in touch with the rest of the army, specially trained soldiers had to carry big radios on their backs. They were about the same weight as a microwave oven.

A WATER BOTTLE You'd probably have to fight in places where fresh water was in short supply. Soldiers often brushed their teeth, shaved and made a cup of tea all with the same cupful of water! Bleurgh!

A SPADE To dig holes to hide in, and also to go to the loo in.

WORLD WAR II FACTS

- The German tanks were called 'Panzers', which means 'armour'.

> In Germany a rhinoceros like me is called a Panzernashorn!

> In the UK a rhinoceros like you is called a Big Twit!

- Churchill had always enjoyed a good battle. When he was a boy, he used to spend hours playing with thousands of toy soldiers on his nursery floor.

- Both sides were proud of how many enemy planes they shot down. The German air force counted 3,058 British planes they had destroyed in the war – truly incredible, especially as the RAF never even had that many!

- The Russian leader, Josef Besarionis dze Jughashvili, changed his name to the catchier Joe Stalin when he was in prison because it made him sound hard. He picked Stalin because it means 'Man of Steel'. Joe was a criminal mastermind with a violent streak. He'd been sent to prison eight times . . . and escaped seven times!

DEFENDING BRITAIN FACTS

■ The British government's evacuation plan, to move 800,000 children out of the cities and into the countryside where they would be safer from bombs, was called **'Operation Pied Piper'**!

■ Evacuees never knew exactly where they were going; they were just told to take enough food for two days.

- Everyone in Britain was given a gas mask in case the Germans attacked with poison gas. The warning signs were oddly nice smells:
  Tear Gas smells like peardrops. **Blister Gas** smells like geraniums. **Poison Gas** smells of mown grass.

- Anti-aircraft guns, called **ack-ack guns**, were designed to shoot German bombers out of the sky. They were ginormous, with fifteen-foot long barrels (more than twice the height of a tall man). They were so big, it took a crew of eleven people to work each gun!

FRENCH RESISTANCE FACTS

- One member of the French Resistance was a middle-aged woman called **Berthe Fraser**. To her neighbours she was just a normal housewife, but in secret she helped British agents working in France. She gave them shelter, arranged transport and safe hiding places, organized meetings and carried messages hidden in her bags of shopping.

- Once, Berthe was asked to help an important British spy travel across France without being detected, so she organized a funeral procession and hid him in the coffin!

- One of the first acts of resistance in World War II was carried out by a group of schoolkids! In November 1940, after the Nazis had taken over France, some French schoolchildren gathered in the centre of Paris and publicly celebrated the defeat of the Germans in World War I.

SECRET HEROES

In World War II many secret weapons were developed for spies and stored in a secret room in the Natural History Museum in London which became known as **'Churchill's Toy Shop'**.

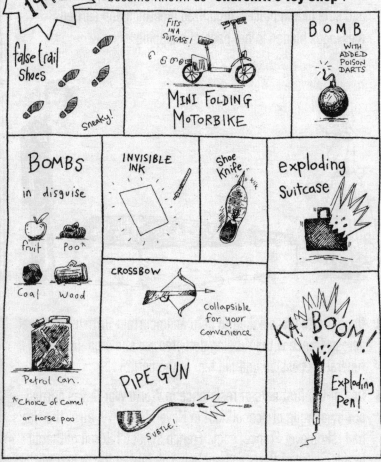

The author Ian Fleming, who wrote the James Bond books, worked with the Special Operations Executive and based his characters on real secret agents!

- **Krystyna Skarbek** was just one of the SOE agents with astounding stories. On one occasion she parachuted into France, chatted up some German guards and persuaded them to release a group of British spies they'd captured. Another time she secretly skied over mountains and through blizzards to get into Poland.

- She narrowly escaped capture by the Nazis several times. Once she pretended to be seriously ill by biting her tongue so hard that she coughed up blood. Another time she was stopped by two German guards at a border crossing and produced two live grenades. When the guards ran away she chucked the grenades at them and escaped across the border!

Why did Stalin get everywhere so quickly?
Because he was Russian.

A FIGHTING FACT

■ Finnish soldiers in the Arctic fought on skis and wore white padded uniforms, which kept them warm and made them invisible in the snowy landscape. They used to sneak up on the Russian troops, attack them and disappear back into the forest.

We are so well hidden in the snow, no one can see us at all!

U(NPLEASANT)-BOATS

■ German submarines were called **U-boats**, and they were hot, damp and cramped. The food on board a U-boat got covered in mould – loaves of bread were nicknamed 'rabbits' because they were so white and furry!

■ U-boats were given the nickname **'swine boats'** because of the smell of all those sweaty sailors who didn't get much chance to wash. When they got to shore, all the bed clothes were burned – they were too filthy to be kept.

Pooh!

■ Ships also used **listening devices** to detect submarines underwater, so if there was a ship on the surface the entire U-boat crew had to be totally silent, sometimes for hours at a time. They could only talk in whispers, and if they flushed the loo by mistake they'd probably be bombed to pieces!

D-DAY FACTS

- **D-Day** was the date when the Allies sent their troops across the Channel to land in Normandy and take northern Europe back from the Germans. The 'D' in D-Day stood for . . . Day! Presumably 'Day Day' would have just been too silly. D-Day is a term that military commanders use for the day an operation would take place – especially if that day has to be top secret.

- To help keep their invasion plans secret, the Allies created a pretend invasion force complete with inflatable rubber tanks and planes, dummy airfields and fake landing craft, and used sound systems on the back of trucks to broadcast the noise of an army on the move. They even broadcast fake radio messages between non-existent ships, while at the same time dropping bundles of tiny metallic strips from aircraft that gave the impression on enemy radar screens of a massive incoming bomber raid far inland. The Germans were totally fooled. In fact, the trick worked so well that when the real invading army landed, Hitler thought it was a diversion from the actual invasion and held off sending his army to stop it.

- The Allied soldiers carried **'magic bullets'** with them for the invasion. 'Magic bullet' was the name doctors used for a special type of medicine – one that was so effective, it seemed to work by magic. It was called penicillin, and before it was invented, lots of people died from small infections. Penicillin kills the bacteria that cause infection, and during World War II, scientists in Britain and America worked hard to produce stockpiles of the stuff. Finally, by D-Day there was enough to treat all the injured Allied soldiers involved in the invasion, which saved thousands of lives!

STIG'S TOP TEN DAFT INVENTIONS

The famous scientist Albert Einstein once said, 'If at first an idea is not absurd, then there is no hope for it' ... but some ideas are more absurd than others. Here are my favourite top ten daft inventions!

Amphibian Bicycle Can Travel on Land or Water

The amphibian bicycle, left, ridden by its French inventor, has its supporting outrigger globes raised so it can be used for land travel

Drawing below, suggests the manner in which the bicycle, pictured at left, would drop the outrigger floats and be supported by them and the wheels in water travel

A HYBRID among vehicles, an amphibian bicycle that can travel on land or water, was demonstrated by its French inventor at a recent Paris exposition. Its wheels are hollow, bulbous floats that, with the aid of four smaller globes on outriggers, sus-

1 THE AMPHIBIOUS BICYCLE – Sounds great, looks ridiculous. A bicycle that can be ridden on water! It was designed by a French inventor in the 1930s, and instead of wheels there were six large flotation balls, which rotated when you pedalled. One puncture and you'd sink without trace.

2 **THE NECK BRUSH** – This torture-like device was developed by a brush company in America in 1950, after a mother said she had trouble keeping her kid's neck clean. It's a large plastic collar with a brush inside, which clamped around the neck and stopped it getting dirty.

3 **THE SELF-CLEANING HOUSE** – Frances Gabe hated housework so much she designed a self-cleaning house! Each room had a box in the centre of the ceiling, which sprayed soapy water everywhere, then gave it a good rinse and blow-dry! The furniture was waterproof, the floors sloped so that water could run off and any delicate objects were protected under glass.

4 **THE SAFETY COFFIN** – A way to avoid the awkward and embarrassing moment when you find you have been accidentally buried alive. Before you were buried, strings were attached to your hands, head and feet, and these were connected to a series of bells. If you woke up, you simply wiggled your hands and feet and alerted passers-by. It came with a

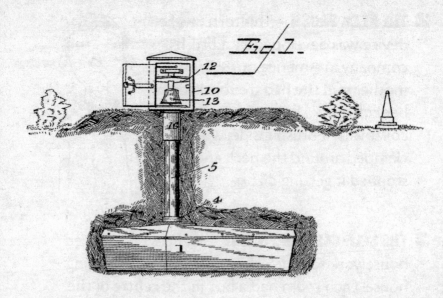

Fig. 1.

handy tube so that air could be pumped in until you could be dug up again.

5 **THE ALARM FORK** – This is a fork with a little alarm fitted in the handle, designed to prevent greedy people overeating. It was equipped with sensors, and if it thought you were shoving too much cake into your face, a red light came on, and an alarm would sound telling you to put down your pudding!

6 **BALLOON SHOES** – John Logie Baird is famous for inventing television, but he also had some total duds. Like his shoes with balloons in the soles, so you could walk more comfortably. When he tried them out, he found walking on balloons was tricky and passers-by thought he was drunk! Then one of the balloons popped and he fell over.

7 THE BABY CAGE – This was developed in the 1930s for people who lived in high-rise flats and wanted to give their darlings some fresh air and sunshine by putting them in a cage and hanging them out of the window! Really lucky children got one with a roof to keep out the rain, snow and bird poo.

8 CLAPPER MITTENS – Not getting enough applause in your life? Try James Crawford's 'Clapper Mittens'. These were basically two lumps of wood strapped to your hands, which you banged together to make a loud noise. Issue a pair to all your friends and get them to whack them whenever you walk past!

9 THE GREENHOUSE HELMET – Short of breath? Breathe in the oxygen given off by plants when you wear the Greenhouse Helmet! This was a sealed plastic dome, designed in 1985, that fitted snugly around the head and contained tiny shelves for plants. It had speakers and a microphone so you could still talk to people – although I'm not sure you'd find anyone who'd want to talk to you.

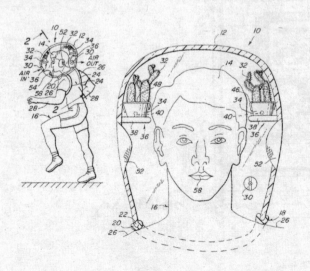

10 **THE LIFE-EXPECTANCY WATCH** – It works out how old you're likely to be when you die, then counts down how long you've got left to the exact day, hour and minute.

That'll keep you cheerful, won't it?

Why did the secret agent stay in bed?
Because she was undercover.

On holiday in Brighton, Winston Churchill and some friends bought some Brighton Rock to eat. Excited, his friends asked Winston where they would go to eat them. He paused to think for a moment, and then said, 'We will bite them on the beaches!'

NITS'S TOP TEN BIZARRE PET INVENTIONS

10 Doggles – Goggles for dogs. They are tinted so they work as sunglasses, but they can also be used with prescription lenses to help dogs with poor eyesight.

Sponsored by

Nagg®

by from nose to tail

9 Pet High Chair – Most pet owners don't want their pets to eat at the table. But for those who do – here's the answer!

8 Cat Toilet Seat – Why not put your cat's litter tray in the bathroom and train it to use the loo?

7 Pet Translator – If you don't know what your pet's trying to tell you, get this Japanese gadget. It translates your dog's barks into messages that appear on a handheld screen.

6 Cat Typing Detector – This detects when your cat is on your computer and locks the keyboard.

5 Dog Perfume – To cover up the usual smell of wet dog and fox poo.

How do I google 'mouse kebab'?

4 **Goldfish Walker** – Ever felt sorry for goldfish going round and round the same old tank? Now you can take them for interesting walks around the local neighbourhood.

3 **Cat Exercise Wheel** – On the other hand, if you have a cat that doesn't want to leave the house, you can give it a run on its very own wheel.

2 **Hamster Cars** – What hamster doesn't dream of cruising along the floor in an open-topped pink convertible?

1 **Bird Nappies** – People may tell you it's lucky to get pooped on by a bird. But they're wrong. It sucks. This handy nappy is for your pet bird – so it doesn't leave any surprises down your back when you let it out for a fly!

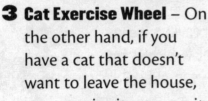

PET FACTS: RECORD BREAKERS

Longest dog tongue: Puggy the Pekinese from Texas has a tongue that is 4.5 inches long.

Most tennis balls in mouth: Augie, a golden retriever, can hold five tennis balls in her mouth at the same time.

Longest cat: Stewie measures 48.5 inches long – or just over four feet (which is the height of an average eight-year-old child!).

Most flying discs caught: Rose the Labrador can hold on to seven frisbees without dropping them.

Most balloons popped: Anastasia the Jack Russell terrier can pop a hundred balloons in 44.49 seconds.

Loudest purr: Smokey the grey tabby cat can purr up to 92.7 decibels, which is as loud as a lawnmower or a hairdryer.

Why is a puppy good at DIY?
Because it's always doing little jobs around the house.

What kind of cat loves water?
An octopuss.

Peewee: I'd like a new fish, please.
Pet shop owner: Sure! Do you want an aquarium?
Peewee: I don't care what star sign it is!

TOP FIVE BIZARRE PETS

5 MONKEYS The ancient Romans used to dress their pet monkeys up in hats and tunics, teach them to play musical instruments and train them to ride goats and throw spears. In medieval times, kings and queens often owned monkeys to show their subjects how rich and extravagant they were. Henry VIII's wife **Catherine of Aragon** got very homesick and kept a monkey to remind her of her Spanish homeland where monkeys lived wild and free.

4 SQUIRRELS There are lots of old paintings of these cute little bundles of fur and teeth with their owners. Often the squirrel is attached to a tiny chain to stop it scampering off. In the 1700s, Americans loved pet squirrels so much that people raided squirrel nests to steal the babies and sell them at the local market.

3 BIG CATS Adult lions and tigers grow to the size of a sofa, eat around 15 lbs of raw meat a day and, to mark their territory, spray wee on everything – including you. Between 1990 and 2011, seventy-five pet owners were killed by their exotic pet animals, twenty-one by big cats alone!

2 HIPPOPOTAMUSES Only a handful of people on earth keep hippos as pets. After all, they're really dangerous! In 2011, a South African man was attacked and killed by a supposedly tame pet hippo, which he had kept for more than five years. Some owners have better luck: the Joubert family in Africa adopted a pet hippo called Jessica, who was separated from her mother and swept into the Joubert's backyard during a flood. They raised her by hand and she became part of the family. She even slept on her own double bed! When she grew up, she had to be moved outside to the patio, but still trotted inside for her nibbles, coffee and massages!

1 **ALLIGATORS AND CROCODILES** Owning a crocodile or an alligator is no piece of cake. They can live for up to fifty years and grow up to 20 ft long. But some people love them: one man in the UK shares his home with a 5 ft-long Caiman crocodile. He has spent thousands of pounds making his house croc-friendly, including installing a special pond and an extra-large cat flap! An Australian woman keeps three pet crocodiles in her home, lets them sleep on her son's bed and takes them for walks. To stop them fighting, each croc has its own pond – one in the lounge, one in the bedroom and one in the bath!

ROYAL PETS

- The Roman Emperor **Caligula** used to feed his favourite horse, Swift, on flakes of pure gold.

Glittery poo – great!

- In London, there was a royal menagerie at the **Tower of London**. It housed lions, tigers, elephants, kangaroos and ostriches. Back in the thirteenth century it even housed a polar bear, which had been given to the King of England by the King of Norway. It was kept on a long lead and was allowed to fish in the River Thames!

The Tower of London

GGRRRR!

HISSS!

SQUEAK!

WHOOP-WHOOP!

ROARR!

WHINNY!

CHIRP!

- **Mary, Queen of Scots** owned over twenty little white Maltese lap dogs. When she was beheaded in 1587, one dog crawled out from between the folds of her clothes, lay next to her severed head and refused to budge.

- **King Henry III of France** owned a staggering 300 tiny dogs. Each time he and his wife Queen Louise went out for their daily walk, they'd take a few of them out in a specially made basket that hung round Henry's neck!

- **Queen Elizabeth of Bohemia** was famous for keeping pet monkeys. People said she liked them better than her own children.

This is great!

I'm not very comfortable.

■ In the seventeenth century, the English **King Charles II** kept lots of little dogs, which went with him everywhere. Not everybody liked them. One visitor complained that the King was always messing around with his dogs instead of paying attention to important royal business! There was one breed of spaniel that King Charles especially liked . . .

The clue's in his name, dummies!

■ **Louis XV of France** became king when he was very young. His mum, dad and brother were dead, so he got extremely lonely. But never mind – at least he had his pet dog. He treated his little four-legged friend like a prince, gave him a velvet cushion for a bed, and a gold collar studded with diamonds. He was just as soppy about his cats.

■ **Ferdinand IV of Naples** filled the rooms of his palace with chickens, pigeons, ducks, geese, canaries, cats and dogs.

Queen Victoria was a big animal lover – one of her earliest pets was a spaniel called Dash. The two were inseparable, and on special occasions she used to dress him in a little jacket and trousers. When she was eighteen, she was made queen, and on the day she was crowned, she rushed back after the ceremony to give Dash his bath. When Dash died in 1840, Victoria had him buried in Windsor Park with a marble sculpture on top of his grave.

- The English **King Edward VII**'s white fox terrier, called Caesar, chewed men's trouser legs and was always running off to hunt rabbits and birds. He once disappeared during a royal visit and a whole police force was sent to find him! When Edward VII died, Caesar was heartbroken and spent days outside his master's bedroom door, whining and refusing to eat. At the King's funeral he was given the honour of walking behind the coffin.

I AM CAESAR I BELONG TO THE KING

- Royal pets can often get away with being really badly behaved. In Germany, **Kaiser Wilhelm II**'s dachshunds snapped at people's ankles, nipped at their clothes, clawed the furniture and piddled everywhere. If anyone complained, the Kaiser just laughed!

Charles XII of Sweden had a favourite cat, which used to lie on his desk and sleep on his papers. Rather than disturb him, the King wrote around the cat, leaving a blank cat-shape on his letters!

- **King Haile Selassie of Ethiopia** kept lions, tigers and panthers, which he allowed to roam through his palace.

- **The Maharaja (or King) of Junagadh** in India owned 800 dogs. Each one had its own room, servant and telephone! In 1922 the Maharaja 'married' his favourite dog Roshanara to a golden retriever called Bobby. The three-day ceremony cost £22,000, and was attended by thousands of guests, including 250 dogs dressed in jewels and riding on elephants!

How was your day, darling?

PET FACTS

TOP FIVE THINGS DOGS CAN SMELL

5 DVDs – Dogs can be taught to smell the material that DVDs are made out of so the police can hunt down fakes. In one police raid in Malaysia, dogs found a pile of pirated DVDs worth over $3 million!

4 Drowned Bodies – Believe it or not, dogs can smell through water, so they're used to recover the bodies of people who have drowned.

3 Bed Bugs – Pest-control services use them to search hotel rooms for bed bugs.

2 Booby Traps – Dogs are used by the army to detect enemy booby traps. They need to be silent in order not to alert the enemy, so they're taught to warn their handlers of danger by crossing their ears or raising the hairs on their necks. One dog was taught to stand up on its hind legs when a booby trap was nearby!

1 Cancer – Dogs can even smell human illnesses! Some have been trained to sniff people's breath and alert them if they smell cancer.

What do cats eat for breakfast?
Mice krispies.

Oh come on, don't be silly. What do cats *really* eat for breakfast?
Miaow-sli!

What goes tick, tick, woof?
A watchdog!

Why do mice like baths?
Because they get squeaky clean!

What's orange and sounds like a parrot?
A carrot!

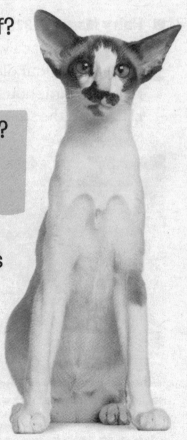

HERO PETS

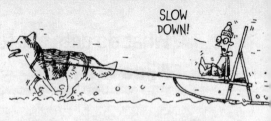
SLOW DOWN!

■ Teams of heroic **husky dogs** saved the kids of Nome, Alaska from diptheria in 1925 by getting medicine. In a race against time, rescuers harnessed teams of huskies, which pulled sleds over 674 miles, through icy blizzards and temperatures of minus 45°C to carry the life-saving medicine to Nome.

■ **Hairy Man:** In 1828 a ship full of Irish immigrants bound for Canada was wrecked in a gale off the coast of Newfoundland. A local fisherman, George Harvey, heard shouting from terrified people clinging to the storm-tossed rocks, and he and his

Newfoundland dogs have got thick waterproof fur and webbed paws. That's why they're such powerful swimmers. They are so strong they can pull twelve people through the water at the same time! In Italy, Newfoundland dogs have been trained to jump from helicopters into the sea to rescue people.

family rowed out to rescue them. But they couldn't get near because of the fierce waves. So their dog Hairy Man jumped into the water and swam to the rocks with a rope between his teeth. A total of 163 people were pulled off the deadly rocks and saved. Well done, Hairy Man.

- **Barry the St Bernard:** High in a remote pass between Italy and Switzerland is a monastery called the Great St Bernard Hospice. The monks there owned big dogs, which rescued people trapped by storms and avalanches. These St Bernard dogs sniffed out injured travellers, dug them out of the snow and lay on them to keep them warm until help came! One St Bernard called Barry saved the lives of over forty people!

What do you call a fish with no eyes?
A fsh!

Which bit of a fish weighs most?
The scales!

HAVE YOU READ . . .

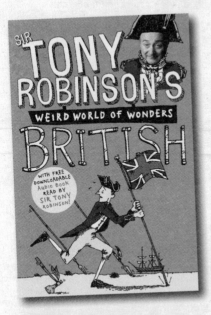

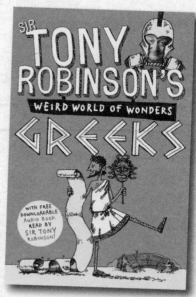

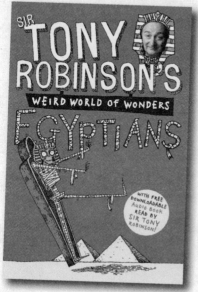

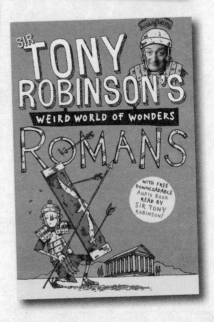

HAVE YOU READ . . .

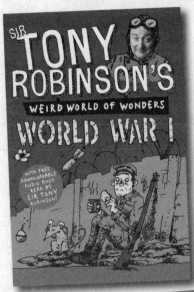

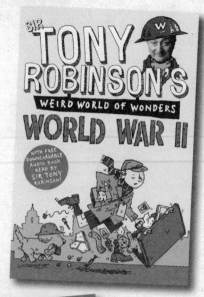

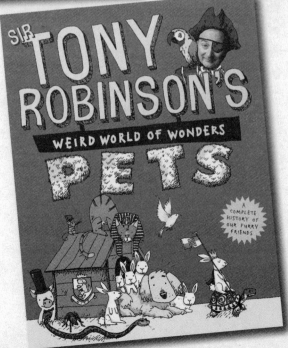

HAVE YOU READ . . .

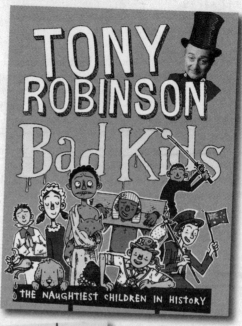

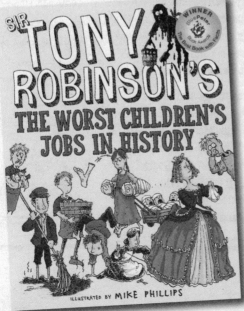

Tony Robinson's Weird World of Wonders is a multi-platform extravaganza (which doesn't mean it's a circus in a large railway station). You can get my World of Wonders game on line, there's a website, ebook, audio versions, extra stories and bits of weirdly wonderful design, marketing and publicity.

In order to get all those things sorted out, I've surrounded myself with a grown-up version of the Curiosity Crew. They are Gaby Morgan, Fliss Stevens and Cheyney Smith (Editorial), Dan Newman, Tracey Ridgewell and Rachel Vale (Design), Kat McKenna (Marketing) and Catherine Alport (Publicity). A big thanks to them all; they are committed, funny and extremely cool.

Tony has to say that otherwise they'd stop work and go home!